T0117204

The Corsage

The Corsage

A bunch of thoughts

KANCHAN SEN SHARMA

PARTRIDGE
A Penguin Random House Company

To order additional copies of this book, contact
Partridge India
000 800 10062 62
orders.india@partridgepublishing.com

www.partridgepublishing.com/india

Contents

(Summary)

A Corsage, is a small collection of flowers which a woman ties around her hand in formal occasions. It signifies the small bundle of happy thoughts, dreams, expectations and love she carries with herself. 'The Corsage' is a small collection of stories written in a poetic form. Each story depicts different strange occurrences of life revolving around human emotions, and how things differ from different perspectives.

Acknowledgements

The most important thing for a budding writer is that small applause they give you when you write the silliest rhyme about the first rains. And that is what my parents, Kallol and Papia Sen Sharma have done splendidly throughout.

Thanks to Sushmita, Riddhiman and Saurabh for telling me that dreams are meant to be fulfilled fearlessly and not to regret about later.

Thanks to the audatious Aparna Manaswini and Abhinav Singh for the photographs which speak my mind.

Lastly, thanks to Shruthee Srinivasan and Mitike Srivastava for being the friends for life.

Mayra's Mirror

She was unearthly,
She was gorgeous,
Everyone described Mayra,
As attractive and vivacious.

People said that her white skin,
Shone like the full moon,
Her sapphire like eyes were,
God's gift and a rare boon.

And everyone who praised her,
Saw her mother working in the house,
Dressed in a long creased skirt,
And a sweaty old blouse,

She was a plump lady,
With a tanned dark, face,
Hair tied up in a messy way,
Hurrying all over the place.

People said that the woman so ordinary,
Was like the thick dark mud,
From where arose the charming,
Daughter like a lotus bud.

The pretty Mayra, drowned in praises,
Admiring herself in front of the mirror,
She had strange queries now,
Her beliefs had started to wither.

In the mirror she saw herself,
How she resembled a ceramic doll,
Was the woman who brought her up,
Her real birth mother at all?

This way veiled in peace and calm,
Many days merrily passed,
Without anyone making the slightest prediction,
That those days of peace were the very last.

Soon there was a war declared,
And the civilians had flee or die to choose,
There were stacks of debris that once were hamlets,
Bloodsheds and hell had broken loose.

People tried to escape at nights,
Houses burnt, families shattered,
Everyone roamed for a safe place to stay,
It was just being alive that mattered.

Mayra had now apparated,
From a rosy to a responsible and cohesive life,
She had a household on her shoulders to carry,
She was now a soldier's wife.

She had rubbed her petal like nails,
On the dirty cooking dishes,
She had spent days and nights working,
To fulfil the domestic wishes,

She had stayed awake in the night until,
The baby had stopped crying,
She had to carry the fruit basket all the way home,
While the clothes were left for drying.

To open the door for her tired husband,
She had to make an abrupt run,
She had always carelessly twisted and tied,
The disturbing long hair into a bun.

After years of hardship and toil,
And sole dedication to her family and husband,
Had made Mayra totally forget about,
An old and once very dear friend.

One day she found the friend in the box,
The old cracked and stained mirror,
And the face which looked back at her,
Was of her beloved, long lost mother.

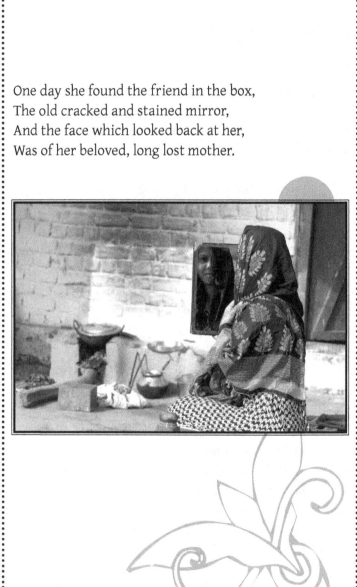

The Vermillion Pride

In India, the Sindoor (Vermillion) is put by married women on their foreheads, still followed as a tradition by even modern families. In rural areas it has a deeper value while in urban areas it's merely a cosmetic.
This is about Bulbul, a little girl of a Widow mother, and her perspective.

Bulbul sat out in the courtyard,
Looking at the sky and the flying kites,
When she saw her aunt SeemaChachi,
Coming to dry her hair in the sunlight.

Her hands full of red tinkling bangles,
Her swaying hair up to her waist,
She looked like a beautiful peahen,
Walking amidst the green forest.

Her eyes lined with dark kohl,
Her Saree with a golden border on red,
Her round, shining face like the moon,
With a bright vermillion mark on her forehead.

Bulbul ran up to her Aunt,
And asked "What's that mark on your forehead?"
Looking down at the curious child,
Wrinkling her nose she shrilly said,

"That's my sindoor on my head,
It's a proof of my womanly pride,
A mark that i have a strong man,
To support me and stand by my side."

Bulbul scratched her head thinking,
While her Aunt strode away,
She sat there, deep in thoughts,
While the other children were busy at play.

Later when her mother returned,
From her work in the late evening,
Bulbul watched her mother carefully,
And observed her deeply thinking,

She was entirely different from her Aunt,
Draped in a white Saree with no bangles,
Her feet on a pair of chappals,
Without any anklets or sandals.

She never talked or laughed much,
Nor was her expression ever proud or stark,
She was nothing like SeemaChachi,
Her forehead had no red mark.

She knew that her mother was an angel,
Who knew to cure people in enchanting ways,
Hence she always dressed in white,
Went to the hospital everyday.

One day when Bulbul climbed up a tree,
To see the eggs which were about to hatch,
Her foot slipped off the weak branch,
And her head got a deep rough scratch.

She sat and cried for a long time,
Badly bruised and covered with dirt,
Till her little friends took her home,
And told her mother how she was hurt.

Her mother made her calmly sit down,
And got the first aid box in a hurry,
She cleaned the wound as gently as possible,
And told her that there was nothing to worry.

But Bulbul looked at her serene mother,
And couldn't prevent her tears from rolling down,
"Be brave Bulbul what's there to cry?"
She asked her child with a frown.

Between several sobs and hiccups,
Bulbul wiped her face with her mother's Saree,
"I am afraid I am not like you Ma!
And I am very ashamed and sorry!"

"You need no one to support and balance,
You walk alone with a clean head,
I always wanted to be like you,
But I became like SeemaChachi instead!"

"She needs a man to support her,
And I am unstable like her or maybe worse,
I fell and got this cut on my forehead,
It's exactly the same as hers!"

Teary eyed Bulbul's mother,
Cleaned her head with alum and water,
She hugged her tight affectionately,
Not knowing what to say to her little daughter.

The Friends

I rushed through the corridor in a jiffy,
I had five minutes to reach my room,
People had again refused to lend me their scooters,
I wished i had a portable magical broom.

I almost slipped on the wet floor,
And i saw the two maids chatting and sweeping,
They always looked so happy together,
While everyone else in the college was complaining and
    weeping.

I stormed ahead talking and trying,
To find someone who could lend me a scooter,
As i turned around to finally leave on foot,
I could hear their chattery laughter.

After many days when i once bunked a class,
I saw both of them washing teacups over giggles,
They talked about some names starting with A,
And about having some stomach wriggles.

One day passing by, i saw one of them,
Walking quietly wrapping a quilt,
I noticed how thin and frail she had become,
Like the garden shrubs beginning to wilt.

I asked her if she was in good health,
She replied like wind passing through a bark hollow,
That she had failed to feel the warmth,
Of motherhood for the third time in a row.

I asked no more and she kept walking,
Her eyes sunk deep into their sockets,
I sighed letting out fog from my mouth,
And moved ahead with my hands in the pockets.

...

Once again i had forgotten to bring a drawing sheet,
After fondling my bag i finally walked out,
The institute had pillars, people and doors,
Everything standing rigid and stout.

Once again one of them was seen mopping the floor,
While the other swayed a broom humming a song,
One remained quiet while the other smiled,
To me, it seemed unlikely and wrong.

How could one sing while the other sulked?
They had to chatter and giggle side by side,
Somehow, i was used to them being alike,
Like the forever smiling maids who stood by the Bride.

As more days passed i was bound to observe them
How gradually one caught up with the other's smile,
Once again their bangles clinked as they worked,
I now could have my peace for a while,

However numbness awaited me,
As i saw them as days moved further,
This time the other friend looked charged up always,
As this time she was going to be a mother.

I wondered how her friend managed to smile,
Battling with her own sad memories of recent past,
Maybe finding self beauty in a friend's mirror image,
That's the true friendship deep and vast.

She would see her friend's cradle,
And buy her little toys made of clay,
While her house had an empty courtyard,
With no one to toddle and play.

I could see how calm she had become,
How only glasses made noise when she washed,
She carefully took her friend back home,
In the evening when the sun blushed.

One day when i met the mother to be,
I saw her beaming at me, loosely dressed,
I congratulated her and smiled telling her,
How she and her husband were so blessed.

She chuckled like a girl and said to me,
That she was single and had no husband at all,
Yet she undoubtedly felt blessed,
That a baby would soon be here and crawl.

Seeing the brightness of her smile i couldn't react,
I didn't know exactly what to say,
Patting the bulge on her stomach,
She slowly kept down the teacup tray.

"She was facing it again and again,
I couldn't see the dark clouds around her any more,
They cracked coconuts on every temple porch,
They went to every doctor's door.

She wasn't sure but I had decided,
That we had to put this dilemma into the tomb,
People sacrifice their lives to friendship Gudia,
I just lent my friend my womb.

Again she made me go dry of words,
Dressed in an oversized dress so austere,
She managed to radiate an angelic light,
That woman did not belong here.

She sacrificed her nine months to pain,
So that her friend's family was completed,
And they swept the floors of that building,
Where for assignments people ditched and competed.

In the grey water of the college sink,
They had found the priceless friendship pearl,
They still come, work and chat together,
Accompanied now by a beautiful little girl.

The Guitarist

The beautiful instrument sat beside my bed,
It's wooden body spreading it's grace,
I picked it up, hung it on my back,
And got ready to begin my day.

With my passion on my back,
And the wind in the flow,
I buttoned my coat,
and pulled my hat very low.

With old boots on feet,
I quickened my pace,
With my identity hidden,
behind the hat like my face.

I placed myself on the railing,
At the west street's end,
So that every passer by could see me,
As the path was about to bend.

I held my guitar like a ballroom partner,
And placed my finger on the string,
There was an imaginary world of melodies,
And I felt like a self claimed king.

A pretty woman saw me,
And looked at me in admiration,
Standing close to my tall shadow,
For some moments she felt the musical sensation.

The next moment she checked her watch,
When she came out of the musical trance,
Without dropping a penny to my bowl,
She whirled away without a further glance.

Next came an innocent child,
And listened to my finger moves,
Then strode his young father,
To see his son in the addictive grooves.

He grabbed the child impatiently,
And told that he was in a hurry,
And that he was late for his work,
And he had a whole lot to worry.

Standing at the Street End,
With no money in my Bowl,
I kept playing the whole day,
Fruitlessly just to please my soul.

Some people were generous to drop a coin,
Some did not even spare a look,
While my fingers bled at the end,
For the painful joy they took.

Then came the new morning,
And i again glanced at my Guitar,
But his time instead of hanging it on my back,
Magnificiently, it sat in my car.

Instead of the shabby brown hat,
I had my dark hair Gelled,
My old and worn off coat,
was replaced by suit, tie and belt.

Instead of the small street end,
I headed for the MNC today,
Instead of trooping in old boots,
I zoomed my sedan all the way.

Grabbing my guitar i walked in,
with my polished shoes hitting the tiled floor,
I walked into the conference hall,
With a man saluting at the door.

People stood up in honour,
But i sat down without a glance,
Took out my Guitar and set myself free,
as my fingers began to dance.

As i finished my performance,
Everyone around stood stunned,
With their mouths slightly ajar,
as if someone had been gunned.

After a moment there was a roaring applause,
For two minutes without a pause.

Then came the pretty woman,
Whom i saw yesterday on the street,
She hastily walked up with a smile,
Her face beaming with a greet.

The man who was getting late for work,
Now stood in front clapping palms,
Then i bowed a little for them,
And a raised hand had made them calm.

The woman was called Rosaline,
And she was my secretary,
While the man Gilbert was a clerk,
Cheering for my musical victory.

They all looked mesmerized by the same notes,
Which I played yesterday on the street end,
Today I was the owner of the place they worked in,
Yesterday I was a poor bloke playing for bread.

People worship you when you have prosperity,
For a penniless, everyone's an atheist.
Tomorrow I shall find a new street to play,
Under old layers of rags covering the Guitarist.

The Worst Singer

Far away amidst the velvety hills,
Enveloped by tall trees of Pine,
There stood a beautiful Temple,
Of the Goddess so holy and divine.

Folklore ran that many years ago,
When a tea gardener's devoted wife,
Had sung a soulful prayer to her,
The idol of the goddess had come to life.

She had raised an open palm,
And blessed the woman of such a power,
That she could light up fire with her voice,
Splash the waters and touch a star.

Since then, every girl around there,
Had this deep in the heart desire,
To stir the goddess with their songs,
And turn her alive in whole form and attire.

Every morning the villager girls,
Would come to the temple and sing aloud,
The sweetest possible incantations,
Reaching melodiously every ear around.

And then a little girl would come,
Every morning with a warm smile,
To sing to her beloved goddess idol,
From her home she would walk up a mile,

But all the women at the temple,
Would yell at her and would scold,
And every morning the little girl,
Would return from the temple's stone threshold.

They said she had a hoarse voice,
And that she sounded like a croaking frog
She would sadly turn away,
And disappear behind the morning frog.

This way the days passed by,
And the prayers were sung every dawn,
Lamps were lit, rituals done,
This way many months were gone.

One night a hermit passing by,
Saw the little girl on her knees,
Singing loudly in her hoarse voice,
Alone in the temple, singing at ease.

It was a chilling cold night of December,
When the temple' steps were covered with frost,
But the girl kept singing with her eyes closed,
He had never seen someone so devotionally lost,

And suddenly the bells rung aloud,
And the dim lamps grew bright,
And the divine idol opened her eyes,
The atrium was filled with unearthly light.

The hermit was stunned and dazed,
He ran up to the temple and fell on her feet,
He felt blessed out of imagination,
He didn't know how to speak or greet,

The goddess smiled and looked down,
At the little girl who had begun to quiver,
"Ask for any wish my dear!"
She said in the most enlightening voice ever.

The hermit was too dazed in her aura,
The little girl stood there timidly,
While finally recollecting his senses,
The hermit asked to the goddess gently.

"you leave me speechless with your flamboyance,
O h my goddess, the motherly, the ferocious,
So many people sang out their hearts to you,
In voices so sweet and so melodious.

But then you chose this very girl,
Who was driven away by all,
Is this out of sympathy my goddess??
These blessings of yours on this creature small."

The goddess smiled and said,
"Sympathy is for those who are weak,
True Dedication and love is the strongest,
And that is only all i seek.

The other women sang to me,
Lit the temple with glowing flames,
Not because they had love for me,
But for recognition and for fame.

They knew how sweet their voices were,
And they sang for me all day,
They never really cared about me,
They cared about what the audience says,

This girl knew she wasn't too sweet,
But she tried her best to sing for her Goddess,
While the rest of the world just displayed their affection,
To true dedication they were completely clueless.

I bless this little girl of such a voice,
That can stir every human soul,
The young girl who loves me immensely,
From her body and heart whole.

The Solitaire's Sulk

It peeped out of the bay window,
To look at the old friend across the pathway,
It always brought joy to it's heart,
That one grey pebble on the roadside array.

Each year this time, it got the chance,
To sit beside the window and gape,
To the old pebble pal who smiled back at it,
Each year, rubbed into a different shape.

It was kicked sometimes by a passerby,
And rolled down to the side of the lane,
While, itself being a solitaire diamond,
Casted dazzling lights on the window pane.

The solitaire looked at the pebble,
As it fell into a nearby puddle,
Splashing water it bounced upwards,
Both the stones burst out into a chuckle.

When the festival of Deepawali came every year,
The only time when the ring was taken out of it's case,
And the sparkling diamond eagerly waiting,
To peep out despite of it's hard silver base.

It wished it could at least once,
Greet it's friend with a gentle knock,
Gaze all night at the sky alongwith,
And meet every other stone, pebble and rock.

The silence of the locker had become unbearable,
The darkness of the case had begun to haunt,
The hundred sharp cuts on it's body,
Has now started reflecting the loneliness taunt.

It fancied sometimes those of it's brothers,
Who had managed to reach out so high,
They gleamed all together joyfully and freely,
Whenever it looked at the dark night sky

It had no dreams of reaching too high,
It wanted no price tag, no shine, no dazzle,
All it wanted was to be the grey pebble,
Who was now getting wet in the droplets of a drizzle.

The wave's Spark

[This is a Goa based poem, a coastal state where people following Christianity as well as Hinduism reside. In India, till date inter community love affairs aren't happily accepted, nor is an independently decision making girl.]

The pressure was getting higher each day,
With every second person complaining,
Some said she was found riding horses,
Some said she danced while it was raining.

Some said she roamed in the evenings late,
Even after the sky fell dark,
Some even claimed that they had seen,
Her hand in hand with Peter Spark.

He felt gloomy inside his own house,
He thought he would take a walk rather,
He got disturbed when he heard things about Lila,
Being the young girl's father.

Walking quietly the middle-aged man,
Reached a spot which gave him peace,
A rocky deserted beach nearby,
Which soothed him with solace and breeze.

He loved to look up at the sky,
Looking at a particular white seagull,
Seeing it he would feel his mood warming up,
Which was nowadays bland and dull.

The white beautiful seagull would,
Swoop down to touch the waves,
And then again soar up high,
Spreading it's wings with mystical grace.

It seemed to have no boundations,
It seemed to penetrate the white clouds,
Noiselessly moving on it's path,
Against the waves' crashing sound.

As the seagull disappeared to the horizon,
He slowly turned around to return back,
Walking silently his mind half lost,
Moving aimlessly on the sandy track.

Lila had been such a fine daughter,
Since she was a small little girl,
But she had always made him run around,
Making his fatherhood twist and whirl.

Too active to be held at one place,
Too mischievous for a girl child,
A very responsible daughter mostly,
At times very bizarre and wild.

But recently she had crossed the line,
Breaking the glass of feminine elegance,
And claimed to be in love with a sailor,
And tested her father's patience,

She called absurdness by the name Love,
Her meaningless defiance and immaturity,
Her father finally decided to marry her off,
To a decent family of the same community.

He knew no matter how much she wailed,
He could no longer be lenient and warm,
It was the time to tighten the grip,
He needed to now be strict and firm.

This way days went by,
Soon was made the scarlet wedding dress,
Where Lila's closet was overflowing with clothes,
Her face was stripped off all the happiness.

One day again taking a break,
Her father walked up to the lonely shore,
To relax himself by looking up,
And seeing the seagull swoop and soar.

Down came the beautiful bird,
From the sky's unknown peak,
To swiftly dip it's head in a wave,
And come out with a fish in it's beak.

And as soon as it glided upwards,
To reach it's undefined heights,
An arrow shot straight to it's wing,
Interrupting the soulful flight.

The man was shocked as he saw the bird,
Falling freely towards the land,
And moments before it was to hit the sand,
The hunter grabbed it in his left hand.

Shocked he stared at the young hunter,
Who stuffed the seagull into a bag,
And the bird's wing peeped out of it,
Like a defeated unfurled flag.

"Wait!" he yelled at the hunter,
Who was just about to turn away,
Running up to the muscular fellow,
He didn't know exactly what to say,

"Son, this is a very angelic bird,
Look at the poetic way it flies,
Look at it's feathered fine wings,
It was born to rule the skies!

Don't kill it for it's meat,
For I will pay you for it instead,
Spare it's life, let it breathe!
Let it's wings again be spread!"

The hunter gave a slight smile and said,
"You feel so much for this little bird,
But wish to make your own daughter a captive,
Isn't that a little absurd??

Wasn't she always born to sing?
Dance, and merrily laugh aloud,
And collect the pebbles of happiness all life,
Taste every cuisine of adventure found?

Why then do you listen to the world?
And make her a captive in her own house,
And wish to turn a happy squirrel,
Into a timid homely mouse?

She needs a man who respects her freedom,
Who accepts the little girl within her,
Who lets her live the way she wants,
Who is exactly insanely joyous like her.

Now take your unconscious bird with you sir,
As I myself don't believe in kill and slaughter,
I am the sailor Peter Spark,
Who's madly in love with your daughter......"

The Red Wine

Sitting in his favourite corner,
Over the glass of blood red wine,
The pub was the very place where,
Rob had seen her for the first time.

Accompanying Alex, the fat girl in the neighbourhood,
Seeing her, he fell in a pleasant hysteria,
Someone said that the girl with Alex,
Was her beautiful elder sister Victoria.

Rob had known that family for years,
And he knew that they had an elder child,
Who studied in another town away,
And that, she was good natured and mild.

But since he saw her in the pub,
After many years when she had returned from the town,
Rob felt the existence of a passionate heart inside,
His world had turned upside down.

He waited for her every evening there,
With the company of his glass of wine,
Awaiting a formal introduction,
Hoping some day he would be invited to dine.

He wished to be that little flower,
Which stuck to her hairbun when she danced,
Sitting there every evening to nightfall,
He smiled at himself and dreamily glanced.

This way passed by many days and weeks,
Since Victoria has come to the place,
But he couldn't even dare to approach her,
Her very sight made his heart race.

One day arrived a long brown envelope,
And Rob looked at it happily,
As it was an invitation for dinner,
From the neighbouring Bernard family.

Finally he could sit and dine with her,
Thought Rob gently unfolding the card,
Till he read that he was invited,
To the elite wedding of Victoria Bernard.

All the dreams like ripples in a pond,
Suddenly turned into hot, dry sand,
He sat stunned for a while there,
Holding the piece of paper in his hand.

How could destiny be so ruthless,
Every ray of love and hope got dimmer,
How could Victoria choose to marry someone,
While he even hadn't got to talk to her

He heard gentlemen talking that she was marrying,
A rich businessman who looked fine,
Every talk about the upcoming wedding,
Made him order more glasses of wine.

After the wedding the Bernard family,
Was last seen moving away in a car,
While Rob lived his solitary life,
Alone, in the dark, crowded bar.

The smoky darkness of the pub,
And the blaring musical noise,
Prevented him from looking at himself,
And hearing is own wounded voice.

3 years went this way for him,
When his life had hours of only work and wine,
When eventually after a prolonged time,
His life got a little bit of a shine.

He had noticed her smiling at him,
Once beside himself sitting with a mocktail glass,
Her golden hair dangled upto her waist,
She said, Sandra was what she was known as.
Rob and Sandra met everyday,
And talked and shared healthy laughter,
And then finally Rob realized the fact,
That he had lost his heart to her.

He told her timidly one day,
That he wished to spend his life with her,
And she just smiled shyly,
And quickly slipped the ring into her finger.

After they had confessed their deep love,
Sandra asked him about his past,
The way she asked him looking at his eye,
He had to tell about his past love at last.

"She went for some rich bloke,
Before i could even talk or woo,
She never even saw my simplicity and love,
After all every girl is not like you."

"As i am just an ordinary clerk,
And he must be earning more than my boss,
She valued his richness more than my love,
That wealthy chap, whoever he was."

"Mark Asher ", said Sandra suddenly,
"Orphaned when he could just crawl on his knees
Worked at a printing press and sold newspapers,
To collect his own school fees.

Grew up and completed his business studies,
Fighting each odd and difficulty,
Had loved Victoria since 8 years,
Since he had seen her in the University.

When finally Mark fought his way,
And owned his own news Agency,
He finally came down to her hometown,
And asked for her hand with all grace and decency.

How hard did you try to get her Rob?
What did u change in yourself, just think,
He improved his status for years and years,
While you didn't even change your drink.

It was me who loved you since i was a kid,
Me, who loved you to the levels of insanity,
I changed even what was god's giving,
I changed my whole appearance and personality."

Rob shocked like hell stared at her,
And asked "Sandra who are you?"
She winked playfully at him "I am Alex,
Alexandra Bernard totally in love with you."

It Was A Bad Day

She had fallen asleep on the table,
Working late on her drawing sheet,
Stains of coffee droplets annoyed her more,
As she struggled to keep it neat.

It was a task to find right clothes in the morning,
When salwar kameez was all you had for option,
Her hair too chose to be too tangled that day,
Everything seemed like a point of deception.

Her work was declared unsatisfactory at the college,
And that she had to redesign the whole stuff,
She quietly rolled it into her holder,
The day was being truly rough.

In the evening she had to meet him,
So she reached the decided location of the date,
She smoothened her hair, checked her phone,
He today was being exceptionally late.

The time went on and on,
But he didn't happen to appear,
Finally she rose and walked off,
Full of outrage, unable to bear.

It was a bad day for him,
The first news he had heard was of Vinay's promotion,
An arrogant junior who was now his equal,
He was in a state of pure agitation.

All the sincerity and hard work paid him nothing,
There were people half talented growing past him,
He did not know what was the scope of his future,
Since morning he was very dull and grim.

On his way out of the office,
They both caught each other's glance,
And then the corridor witnessed a short curt row,
How could Vinay miss that day any chance.

He had to meet her in the evening,
When he remembered he hurried out to the parking way,
But a flat tyre of his bike had put,
A cherry on the salad of bad luck of the day.

So he hurried to a nearby flower shop,
Which was just about to close,
And he requested the florist to give him,
Any bouquet, pansy petunia or rose.

The florist said that he had just one last bouquet,
Which a little boy standing nearby had bought,
He asked the boy a few times to give the flowers to him,
But the boy gently kept saying that he could not,

Baffled and tired he lost his cool,
And grabbed the boy by his little throat,
Scared out of his wits the boy quickly,
Surrendered those flowers to the man in the Black coat.

...

The boy kneeled down and said to her,
"Trust me this day was really harsh,
First of all i was pretty late at the garage,
And i couldn't repair much of the cars.

And i met this angry, young man!
Who snatched away your flowers i had managed to buy,
Sorry i just couldn't bring anything,
On your birthday but please don't cry.

I'll work hard, earn a lot and you'll see,
I'll get you a corsage like those rich Memsahibs,
And maybe buy myself a shawl,
This cold has been freezing my ribs.

He sat quietly and lit the half melt candle,
In front of the stone grave of his sister,
And kept talking about the whole day for hours,
And the unbearably cold weather.

The Art Attack

He moved his hand nervously again,
Through his well gelled hair,
Then looked back at her dark brown eyes,
Sitting on an uncomfortably cushioned chair.

"I had some work here nearby in the town,
So your mother asked me to pay a visit,
So tell me about yourself Jiniya,
I heard you're a good artist, is it?"

She looked at his greasy hair,
And his immense attempts to look decent,
She noticed the pride of richness in him,
And his fake American accent.

"Oh no, i am no great Artist!"
She said with a forced out giggle,
"I can just use my imagination,
And can stroke with the paintbrushes at little."

He said" You don't need any goddamn art!
To be a dedicated homely spouse,
But still i appreciate your talent Miss,
Can you show me the paintings in your house?"

Hearing this Jiniya smiled sugar coated,
"Of course, that would be my pleasure,
Ours has been a family of artists,
Our paintings are our prized treasures."

She asked him to accompany her,
And lead him to the studio at the back,
Where hung numerous paintings,
And canvases stored in a stack.

He casually looked at her paintings,
And mechanically uttered some words of praise,
Till his eyes fell on a corner painting,
Which looked like framed in the olden days.

"Who's that gentleman in the painting?"
He asked pointing at it straight,
She turned around and told him,
"That's Kunwar Baldeo Singh's portrait"

"He was my great grand father's brother,
A very short tempered and violent man,
Nobody wanted to keep his picture,
As he's said to bring curse to the clan."

She said" we didn't talk much about him,
His tale was unpleasant and gory."
But he suddenly looked all interested,
"Jiniya, i wish to know the whole story."

"Okay, i'll tell you if you suggest,"
She said, finally giving a sigh,
"Baldeo Singh wanted to marry off his sister,
And his expectations were quite high,

His sister wasn't beautiful at all,
So no rich man wished her as a wife,
Tired of rejection from everywhere,
His sister one day took her own life.

Baldeo Singh's world had shattered,
So did his hopes and his pride,
He swore to god that he won't let,
Any girl in the family be a bride.

Till today my Aunts are unmarried,
His terror has spread like wild fire,
They say he still lives to kill the suitors,
He had eventually turned into a vampire.

But i don't believe in this story,
I think it's a family rumour mere,
I'll go and get the supper ready,
While you see the paintings stacked in here,"

Saying this she left him there,
In the studio deep in thoughts,
After looking again at the portrait,
He started seeing the painted pots.

The pot which he was looking at,
Smashed on the floor as he saw the window,
His heart beat against his chest,
Seeing a ghostly figure in a moon's glow.

His breathing seemed to cease abruptly,
His heart sank like a shipwreck,
He looked terrified at the portrait,
Dreadfully once again to check.

He stumbled back away from the window,
And landed on the floor with a thud,
As the same pale man in the portrait,
Walked towards him, his lips smeared with blood.

Baffled, he got up and blasted the door open,
And ran out scared and turned white,
He ran and ran and didn't look back,
Till he reached his car outside.

Jiniya went back to the studio,
And opened the French window wide,
"Who was that man Jeeni??"
He asked surprised stepping inside.

"Another suitor, that portrait saved me from,
Again worked my silly little plan,
Thank god you look so similar to grandfather,
And u look scary Brother, after eating a paan."

In India, we are unique, the way we arrange love for our youth and how their weddings become way more than just a ritual in front of God to tie the knot of love.

Love Aftermath

The scarlet roses dangling in the hall,
And the diamond ring sparkling and small,

Reminded me of the starry night,
When i lost my heart amidst candlelight.

How nervous i was, with a shaking heart,
And evryone so concious for a perfect start,

How daintily i was dressed up,
and my hair which was mostly messed up,

Now swayed straight free from tangles,
While my hands crowded with jingling bangles,

I left the house feeling a bit numb,
with all the fears of saying something dumb,

As i finally walked down the stairs,
to look at the elegantly placed tables and chairs,

And then i felt as if my running sweat froze,
as from the corner a young man rose,

Neatly suited and as tall as palm,
Beholding a pleasant smile so calm,

He welcomed me with gentle eyes,
Throwing a flirty look in polite dsiguise.

As i gently placed myself,
on the chair he had already pulled,
With strange feelings and weird emotions,
My mind was so very full.

But slowly as i felt more settled,
in his romantic aura with lingering fragrance,
I felt worda flowing out of me,
and i felt no more nervous and tense.

It was his cool lopsided smile,
which worked for me like intoxicating wine,
Coz it made me pretty frank,
and i unfolded many dreams of mine.

It was surely this hunk to blame,
Or the sensuous candle flame,
Or maybe his eyes bright and gleaming,
Which left my breath hot and steaming.

In my dark and dim youth,
He came like a refreshing Dawn,
And i, defeated, told myself,
Belle!your heart is surely gone.

And then we walked hand in hand,
Like two mixed tides hitting the sand.

And soon the Joyous family members,
of our family and our clan,
Were set up in tedious work,
With a perfect wedding plan.

And soon i found myself,
under many elder and examining eyes,
And was bombarded with strange questions,
cold and sharp like Glacier Ice.

There were queries about my eyesight,
About my abilities of Maternity,
And whether I was in a relationship before,
Ensuring my secured Virginity.

Questions were asked to my father,
Which he answered with great politeness,
But the striking gusts of queries,
somehow seemed to dim his brightness.

How old was our ancestral house,
How many acres we owned of land,
Could we afford the Flamboyant celebration,
How much cash we had in hand.

I listened with a bowed head,
to the proceeding interrogation,
i could see the pride in their eyes,
and their burning desperation.

I tried to recall my Love,
and his loving and caring looks,
My thoughts were interrupted by a question,
about my talent as a cook,

While the inquisitive elders,
stood around like towering trees,
I tried to recall his affection,
and the soothing warmth of his squeeze.

And then they wanted to make,
a very detailed observation,
about our property and land,
and every bit of our possesion.

The same was from our side,
during our turn to pay the visits,
Lots of observation and criticism,
About their abilities and limits.

In all these days, i and my Love,
Could just exchange a few comforting looks,
While the stress of so much to be done,
Haunted our minds like spooks,

Criticisms from nosey Aunts,
Itchy complains from distant brothers,
Money flowing like tap water,.
To show, none was less than the other.

Huge amounts of gifts and sweets,
Sweating us, tiring our bones,
And the sky scraping expanses,
drowning us in massive loans.

Within some childhood buddies' Old friendship,
I finally got through the days of hardship.

Now finally Jewel loaded,
with evry eye goggling at me,
I sit in the hall worrying about,
the expectations that lie on me.

I looked at my tired sweetheart beside,
and he gave me a smile faint,
I wondered if he could see my real face,
Underneath the shiny layers of paint.

All we wanted was a bit of peace,
Brought in by some imaginary Dove,
We thought ' Was so much required?
Just to commit our sweet little Love"

Scars of Love

They laughed at me as i walked,
Down the busy, buzzing lane,
Some referred to me as 'The Ugly Man',
Some suspected me to be insane,

Young girls slid away from me,
To avoid any physical contact,
And as i did always i just kept walking,
Now being used to such an impact,

Slowly walking ahead i came,
In front of a small parlour,
When i saw a young man sitting,
In it with an expression of guts and valour,

A small, pointed metallic machine,
Seemed to drill over his muscular arm,
Despite of the immense pain,
He tried to look strong and calm.

He had in his eyes, the look of pride,
As the machine inked to engrave a word,
He looked at the name written in the tattoo,
And wiped off the little droplets of blood,

Struck he was by the Girl's love,
He didn't bother tattooing is a sin in Christianity,
Yet no one will ever think it as obsession,
Or any kind of childishness or insanity.

Leaving the young man with his scar,
I moved ahead on my lonely way,
And there was a sudden downpour,
So i had to find a shed to stay.

The shed cast a darkness hovering over me,
Hence the people couldn't any longer see my face,
Everyone stood clustered to protect from the drops,
It was a crowded little place,

Smiling at herself in her mind,
A young newly wed bride stood,
She still had the mehendi designs on her palms,
She was using a bright red stole as a hood.

Staring at nothing and a little lost,
Wandering in some sweet daydream,
As every raindrop slid down her body,
She felt her man's warmth turning it into steam,

She could still feel his nails on her neck,
She recalled the robust and strong embrace,
The way he made her sink into his love,
The way they moved with utmost grace.

Be it the scratches of nails on her long neck,
Or the designs of henna all over her hands,
All the scars of her love made her feel proud,
Even though they were like writings on the sand.

Leaving behind the dreamy young girl,
I decided to go ahead in the rain,
Remembering that night of my doom,
My mind was still bruised with pain.

The night of the end of my handsome face,
The night of the end of my youthfulness,
The night which left no one,
But the moon as the only witness.

The last night of my bravery,
Which turned me from jewel to trash,
My last night as an officer,
The night of the airplane crash.

The deep wounds on my body and mind,
Left me bereft of health and power,
I came down crashing on a parachute,
And left me with paralysis and scars.

I wonder if the world thinks,
That the scars of true love are absolutely fine,
If the man and the girl can be proud of their scars,
Why can't i be proud of mine??

The Precious Advice

She tilted her neck to the back of the seat,
Looking at the rays entering faintly,
Her mind thinking about the problems,
Her family had been facing recently.

With the untimely rains ruining the orchards,
And the family business facing a trough,
There was a little shortage now,
And the going was a little tough.

Right from her childhood to the salad days,
She never shopped much nor had the jewellery cravings,
She never wished to have expensive clothes,
She believed in making gradual savings.

But she had cousins who either gambled,
Or spent immensely on shoes or a gown,
Looking out of the train's window,
She felt a bit lost and down.

A gentleman who sat infront of her,
Right from the very first station,
Slowly folded his newspaper into half,
And started a casual conversation.

"Hello madam, My name is Jayanto,
And i am going to the city for a job interview,
I live with my mother and beloved sister,
And may i know a little bit about you?"

She noticed the handsome carvings of his face,
Which seemed to vaporize her inhibition,
"Hello my name is Goyna Mujherjee,
And i am just returning from an art exhibition."

He told her how much he needed a job,
But still, he tried to struggle happily,
While she told him about her dull life,
And several tiffs and issues of her family,

"these exhibitions of modern art don't interest me,
But being eldest of the cousins i had to accept the invitation,
It was my sister who got me all dressed up,
I never even cared to check my reflection."

He said," Never think too much about money Madam,
It's all about how we look at the things,
Think positive and everyone lives the life of royalty,
And we all are self claimed queens and kings,

I always imagine that i am a rich man,
And i try to see everywhere a veiled treasure,
Try to look at everything like it's precious,
You don't know that child like pleasure!

Appreciate everything my lady,
Appreciation is a true art",
Saying that, he pointed outside,
At two children sitting on an open cart.

"I would say they are on a royal carriage,
Out on a picnic in the evening hours,
Giggling, laughing and shrieking with joy,
Way happier that you and i are."

Next he pointed at a young girl,
Who on her head carried a pot of milk,
"I would say looking so pretty at work,
Her plain dress is surely made of silk."

Goyna couldn't prevent a smile,
As he pointed at the window pane,
"Are they less beautiful than diamonds?"
He asked showing the droplets of rain,

"This is an old watch of my father"
Pulling it out of his pocket he told,
"But looking at the emotional value it has,
I would call it more valuable than Gold."

Tucking her hair behind her ear,
Her lips parted into a smile,
"You are a very nice man Mr. Jayanto."
She said impressed by his style.

"I would say Miss Goyna that your hair,
Is beautifully entwined with natural flowers,
But to me it looks like a precious Tiara,
Whose amethysts and diamonds shine like stars!"

"You are such a graceful lady Madam,
Just one last thing i would notify,
You own a smile that can light up all the compartments,
You don't need any jewellery to beautify."

Every bit of pensiveness in her mind,
Disappeared into thin air like vapour,
Finally the gentleman looked away,
And hid himself behind the newspaper.

She opened her eyes when he shook her,
As she has slowly dozed off,
He told her that her station had arrived,
And raised his hat to see her off.

While getting down from the train,
She saw herself in the window glass,
The flowers on her hair looked fragile,
He had appreciated them with such a class.

On reaching home she looked happy,
Wanted to tell her people about the surprise Mister,
When the mahogany door finally opened,
She was greeted by a stare from her sister.

"My god Goyna where have you been?
And who was the fellow passenger there?"
She looked at her sister surprised,
As she came and examined her hair.

"You have lost our family tiara Goy!!"
She saw her eyes getting engulfed in terror,
"I placed it on your hair this morning,
How would you know, you never saw the mirror!"

Doctor Tony Asra's Tale

She stared for long at the ceiling fan,
Secretly wishing there was a rope she could find,
Everything that lay around her bed,
Screamed out suicidal thoughts to her mind.

Her fat body now seemed like a burden,
A heap of flesh that everyone wished to dump,
Every wound in her body was a hole in her soul,
Every word in her throat stuck to form a lump.

What if she had tried to kill herself?
The world never lets her live anyway,
They taunt you when you smile, poke you when you're quiet,
They always have something to say.

There was a soft chime as the door opened,
And came in the doctor with a note pad,
The aura she carried around herself,
The most beautiful eyes in the world she had.

Even the suicidal thoughts calmed down a bit,
As the doctor's smile spread like a sun beam,
Her voice rang in the ears like some hilly music,
Which seemed to suppress every dark, painful scream.

"You look tired Ahana, the sweat on your forehead,
You don't look like you have had a sleep."
She sat beside her bed as she said,
Her voice all so melodious yet deep.

"I don't wish to live this life Dr. Asra,
I don't know why it's so difficult to understand,
I have tried once and i will keep trying till i succeed,
The trigger is always in my own hand."

The words sounded so battered and crumbled,
That she gently placed her hand on her shoulder,
"They laugh at me all the time Doctor,
They say my body looks like a big boulder.

I am sick of the muffled giggles in the classroom,
Tired about the taunts about my size and complexion,
But how would you even remotely feel my pain,
You're a woman made by god, to all levels of perfection."

She looked away from her, out of the window,
Unable to bear her eyes' mystical effect,
Her smile made regular effortss to outshine the darkness
in the room,
Her eyes could mould anyone's intellect.

"I see that you have already decided to die,
You'll continue hurting yourself and make it gory,
I'll make no futile efforts to change your mind,
I'll just tell you a long lost story.

The deep wounds on your body remind me of a tale,
Of someone who slept in the barn with the cattle,
Her mornings were a regular struggle for food,
Her night was a dark and dingy battle.

Orphaned as a baby the little girl had,
Just the thatch of the barn to shade her childhood,
Only trees fed her fruits like a loving mother,
No one made her hair and no one ever would.

She waited patiently every evening,
As the golden hay turned into brown strands after the sun,
When bunches of children came near the barn,
To play on the fresh grass and have fun.

She would run up to them and merge,
Like stream water merged into the ripples of river,
She was the fastest to run, the last to get tired,
She splashed water with her feet in the freezing cold winter.

She waved her fingers on a fallen leaf,
And gradually it would turn green from brown,
She would jump from branches like a bird's flight,
And fetch fruits for the children waiting down,

The children loved her and no one cared,
Where she lived and who was her family,
But every night they would go home and tell,
About their friend who could do things magically.

"Mother today she made a bamboo bend,
With just one finger she's so strong!
Today she made the peacock dance,
By singing a mesmerizing, enchanted song."

She looked at the stars sitting alone,
As she sat in the barn's flickering lamp's light,
Every child she played with must be at home,
With a beautiful mother wishing them good night.

One day during the play they saw some blue berries,
Shiny like sapphires dangling from a vine high,
Some children begged her to get them the bunch,
As she was the only one who could fly.

Listening to them she swiftly jumped,
From one branch to the other like a Frisbee,
She caught those bunches in her young hands,
And swooped down holding a vine of a tree,

The children looked at the sapphire berries,
And swallowed them in excitement and haste,
She saw them as they gobbled all the berries,
And spat them out, disgusted by the taste.

...

It was midnight and she sat singing,
Softly feeling the wind on her face,
When she saw some lanterns and mashaals coming,
Towards the barn in a steady quick pace,

There was a crowd of people storming with sticks,
With faces covered in fear and terror,
The sky too turned dark and cloudy that night,
Reflecting the villagers' mind states like a mirror.

She scared, crouched down and blew off the lantern,
And peeped out to see the raging human hounds,
"Don't go too much further" someone shouted,
"It might be a cursed ground."

"Where is she?" howled an angry villager,
"She isn't allowed to take one more breath!"
"The Tohni, the witch! Who fed cursed fruits to our children!
And made them so sick, they're close to death!"

The hay on the ground felt like needles,
The pleasant air began to chill and freeze,
She was so scared she felt a moving vine,
Crawl inside her body and her heart felt seized.

The villagers had heard about the special girl since long,
But had they predicted this was to come on their way?
They should have realized she was not a little girl,
But a dark sorceress joining their children in the play.

They finally dared to come close to the barn,
Yelling out swearing for the Tohni inside,
The noise and the mashaals got the cattle get scared,
They began to rush here and there in fright.

Her face, wet with tears and dry of color,
She covered her head from being smashed by a hoof,
While they kept hurling stones at the barn,
And threatened to burn the thatch roof.

The villagers, reluctant as they were so many cattle,
Or they would have burnt the whole place to ash,
Finally she managed to get up and run,
As the stones begun to hit and crash.

Struggling and panting she pushed her way,
To the backside of the barn which had a gate,
While the villagers started surrounding the whole place,
Desperately like a scavengers' brigade.

Quick as a squirrel, she ran towards the woods,
Leaving behind the murderous deluge,
And that was the beginning of her long lasting run,
And her journey for a home and a refuge.

She ran and ran cutting through the wind,
From village to village, veiling her identity,
And the same accusations and stones hurled at her,
While she tried to defend her deeds and integrity.

Tired of running and fighting for herself,
The girl almost reached a state of despair,
The world had thrown so much harshness at her,
That her wounds were beyond any repair.

One day when she finally stopped treating,
Her abilities as curses and flaws,
She finally decided to stop fleeing from reality,
And readily accept who she really was.

She knew she had powers,
Of not just running fast and leaving things behind,
But also to read people's emotion with fingers,
She could give them a peace of mind.

Being called a witch and Tohni through the years,
She knew one thing for sure,
That whoever she was, she had to adore it,
And stop pretending to be ordinary and pure

Forgetting the past she started practicing,
Her sorcery as she was meant to,
Completely drowning herself in her passion,
It was a different world she went into."

The Doctor smiled at her as she said,
"And then i started using my conjuring eyes,
I studied psychology to the depths of fathoms,
Used my powers to summon and hypnotize.

I sensed people's deepest fears and horrors,
And made all my efforts to cure and heal,
Never again i put my strengths,
And powers behind a false image's veil.

I even accepted what people called me,
I accepted their accuse of Tohni as Tony,
And changed the blaring noise of my life,
Into a beautiful heart touching symphony.

If they laugh at you then don't feel offended,
That's the world's trick to create a mess,
Once you accept it and start laughing at yourself,
There's nothing to come between you and your success."

The sorceress got up and smiled a good bye,
And the girl on the bed was left deep in thought,
Suddenly everything in her life seemed crystal clear,
She felt no marks, no wounds no spots.

From suicidal her tendencies turned to victorious,
As she let the world laugh at her and shone,
As Ahana left the psychiatrist's ward,
She became the best lady comedian ever known.

The Actress

Her petite body leaned on the sofa,
As she re read her lines again, and again,
Trying to sound more confident each time,
From inside, she was going insane.

Why did it seem so hard this time?
She always had her dialogues on her thumb,
Unlike this time, when she couldn't feel them,
Her face like her mind, looked vaguely numb.

She had flawlessly uttered romance,
They said she had love under her eyelashes,
Dressed in gowns whenever she went outside,
Was surrounded with applause and camera flashes.

For the first time in her career she felt worn off,
She sent for some apple cider and ice,
When the director entered her vanity he could see,
The distress in those dark blue eyes.

"I know it's a task for you Math!" he said,
"Playing a lady dacoit, so tough and bold,
Where there are no fragrant lines to utter,
All's there is, is being violent and cold"

"But I chose you for this role of KaalRaatri,
As I saw the ignition that's inside,
I realized the vigour and power inside you,
Which this pretty doll like face hides.

You must feel the character from your heart,
Math, do anything it needs to succeed,
Feel the character in your blood and veins,
That is the hour's dire, strong need."

She stared at the papers as he left,
At the inhuman coldness of those words in cursive,
The very distant smell of the character,
Made her feel grim, and pensive.

The words of the director echoed in her head,
How she was to feel it in her heart,
And suddenly she knew, she had to go there,
Where Ratri's life story took it's start.

...

The dark linen stole covered her face,
The shawl and the boots completing her dress,
She strode off away from the theater,
And from the vanity air full of stress.

She decided to plunge into the woman's life ripples,
And understand the heart where violence abursts,
In black robes she stealthily walked into,
The darkest streets of the city's outskirts.

She could see a few other women there,
She could sense in their walks, their fears,
She observed the people passing by her,
As the wind howled in her ears.

As the night grew the women disappeared into homes,
While men roamed around looking darker and tall,
She crept up to the side of a house,
And put her ear along the wall.

She could hear drunk abuses of a man,
And crashing of plates on the floor,
The faint sobbing of some little girl,
The slamming of a heavy wooden door.

She moved ahead to the next house in the street,
And heard the snoring of a man,
While his daughter worked on the dishes alone,
Rubbing her gentle hands on a frying pan.

She got lost into what she saw,
Her thoughts in her mind whirled and twisted,
Was this a parallel world around her?
Which she never knew existed.

She had played roles in silk gowns,
And won each time a prestigious award,
While the real women struggled for rags,
Their lives were so contrary and hard,

In the world so dark where the only light,
Is the fire of your kitchen's stove,
Where you are denied even the right to breathe,
And trampled before you rise above,

Mathily turned around astonished,
As she felt a hand on her back,
Covering the remaining crescent of her face,
She stared at the men who stood like a wolf pack,

They wondered her dare to be out so late,
They looked at her like she was a prey,
She read their inhumanly eyes,
All emotionless cold and grey,

They grabbed her wrist as she tried to move,
She could feel the negative vibes on her skin,
As one of them came closer to her,
She could inhale the smell of lust and gin.

With a rush of reflex she turned around.
And with an outburst and tolerance strife,
Straight she sent across his belly,
Her shining silver folding knife.

Down as he fell she pulled it back,
And raised the blood smeared knife to the air,
"I won't hesitate to do this a hundred more times,
Do you still wish to touch me? Wish to dare?"

Shocked by the impact they stood frozen,
She felt no pain, no fear, no remorse,
A part of her was stunned herself as she heard,
Her own voice so loud and hoarse.

Her guards ran to her to the rescue,
While the wind around stopped in her enthrall,
As she walked out of the street with them,
She became a completely different person overall.

...

After days finally arrived the Auction show night,
When people flocked the rows of the theater,
The co actors rehearsed their lines backstage,
Each moment to sound better and better.

Dressed in black corseted robes,
Mathily looked at her chivalrous reflection,
Eyes, as cold as frozen freckles,
Lips pursed up to the level of perfection.

For the first time holding a pistol on stage,
Speaking like a slaying dacoit and a psychotic thief,
She yelled out her soul to the air,
Her voice, hoarse enveloping a core of grief.

As it ended, she strode off the spotlight,
The audience sat in silence for the moment's pause,
As they returned from her enigmatic trance,
There was the most thunderous applause.

He ran backstage to look for her,
As his head rose with pride and honour,
Till he saw the Chairman come to him,
With a pale face and look of horror,

He ran with him to the auction vault,
To see the security guard stabbed on the floor,
Which once was full of antique jewelry,
Now stood all empty with an open door.

As he read the folded note left there,
In the vault's white lighting,
"Finally awake with the inner Rebel within."
Was scribbled in Mathily's dainty writing.

Superstitions

Ignoring the little cat crossing the road.
And zooming ahead on his carefree ride,
Overlooking the little temple on the porch,
Wearing his shoes he continued the stride.

He passed under a dangling string,
Of dried up chillies and lemons,
Twisted the door knob with a holy sign,
Meant to keep out the paranormal demons.

He dropped himself on the disfigure couch,
And the slim LED TV became alive,
Passing through some religious channels,
He finally came to the sports channel line.

With his feet on the mahogany table,
And his eyes on the lush playground,
He yelled for his mother to get him food,
As he felt as hungry as a hound.

In a while a serene lady in a sari,
Appeared with a plate in her bangledhands,
Keeping the food she stood aside,
Watching her son's coloured hair strands.

"What's it that makes you so defiant,
And repulsive towards our cultures ?
Or was there any loophole we left,
In your upbringing and nurture?"

Stone deaf to any argument,
He ignored his mother's advisal array,
Till the lady gave up for the time,
And decide to better walk away.

Observing this from her room,
She silently came up to her brother,
While his eyes were fixed on the screen,
His hands moved from one sandwichto the other.

She sat beside him and kept,
A glass of water with floating ice,
The very stubborn disbelief towards all,
Reflected in her brother's very eyes.

"Seems you had a row with her again,
About the little things from you she wants,
I just want to know why you prefer this disbelief,
Despite of the daily tiffs and taunts?"

Finally looking away from the television,
He decides to give his needed responds,
"yes I don't believe in the crossing cats,
And waking up early to see the upcoming dawns."

"I don't believe in worshipping a stone,
And following faith like a sighted blind,
Because all this culture stuff in nothing,
But superstitions accumulating one mind."

listening to this his sister smiled,
"my brother I don't ask you to be blind
But just that you can't see through the figure,
It doesn't mean there's no road behind.

"the belief of the cat crossing the road,
Makes people conscious during drives,
And though you believe it's a time wastage
But its tends to save many animals lives.

"if you had a little care for the temple
You would have left your shoes there down,
That would have saved this antique table.
From the mud from various parts of this town.

"Bowing your head to the almighty,
Doesn't makes you a helpless slave,
Nor does it maks you a part of any
Supernatural or staunch enclave"

"it just gives you the courage and faith,
To go through the hard times and survive,
It also gives you the necessary fear,
Which ceases one's over confidences to strive,

Unmoved by his sister's logics,
He had already stated his decision,
That he never was and would be
The part of any goddamn superstition.

Giving a sigh the finally got up,
And gathered his empty plate and all.
And was about to leave when.
Suddenly her bother gave her a call.

"do you mind to stay here more?"
He said suddenly with a voice make over,"
"Actually you seen to be lucky for India,
14 runs in a single over!!

The Jewellery Shoppe

She glanced satisfactorily at her masterpieces,
Walking through the alley of her shop,
Smiling at every detail on the accessories,
Like a farmer looking at his ripened crop.

How the intricate wines of silver and gold,
Merged into each other like Dawn and mist,
How beautiful they could make it look,
As a bracelet when tied around a wrist.

Her casual stroll came to a halt,
When the door chimes made a tinkling sound,
And a middle aged man walked inside,
In a black coat and looked around.

"How may I help you sir?"
She said in her professionally sweetened tone,
"Get you a pretty neckpiece for your lady,
Or an elegant tiara studded with stone."

The man kept gazing around the shop,
Till he finally looked at her to say.
"I'm looking for something for my wife,
To present her on her birthday."

Heena looked at the man carefully,
He looked quite well off by his array,
"If you wish for the finest gift for yours wife,
You're at the right place I must say."

"I have the best carved chokers in town,
Earrings that would make look like a doll,
Hairpins, that when put in the hair,
Can make them look like sparkling waterfall.

The man kept looking and looking everywhere,
He passed brooches, tiaras, bracelet and a crown,
There was some dissatisfaction in his eyes,
That made Heena restless and frown.

Thousands of people had visited her shop,
And everyone to some extent, had given appreciation,
Unlike this man with a distinct coldness,
Absorbed in his own observation.

"I may be able to help you out sir,
If you be a bit specific about what you want,"
She said waving a hand around,
At the numerous jewelleries she possessed to flaunt.

I could take any jewellery for her,
Anything that has got the proper charm,
But I see nothing here matches her beauty,
Nothing half as graceful as warm."

Heena thought that his statement and sudden departure,
Was definitely surprising and a bit curt,
She didn't know why he left her affected,
Why was she being so professionally hurt.

"He was just another man with no sense of fashion,"
She said to herself leaning on the table,
"After all where could a woman be around?
Whose beauty makes every jewellery unmatchable?"

To her surprise the man again came,
To her shop the next week, with a hopeful face,
"I know you're the best in the town,
I believe you must've got something in these days."

Heena showed him all the new collection,
Kept blabbering about each piece for long
And the man kept walking slowly with her,
Like listening to some monotonous song.

He had by now seen everything in the shop,
And glanced the collection as a whole,
Again no jewellery seemed to please his eyes,
No design seemed to touch his soul.

He was about to turn away once again,
Out of the door to the open sky,
When suddenly he stopped himself,
Seeing something from the corner of his eye.

He walked slowly towards what he saw,
And Heena curiously followed him,
Finally he pulled out a pulled out a bunch of glittering bangles,
Which were kept in a cardboard box so dim.

With shiny eyes he picked them up,
And slowly muttered the word, wow!,
"How much will these cost me Madame!"
He said, looking happy for the first time till now.

Suppressing her laughter she said to herself,
"leaving all the unique in gold, silver and brass,
Here comes a fool with a handful of coins,
To find his fantasy in bangles of cheap glass.

"You may take these free of cost sir,
As that saves my dump box from overflowing
For if this compliments your wife's beauty.
I bet she must be quite flashy and glowing.

"I would've spent a fortune for this."
He said putting a hand in his coat,
"Anything for my Maria in this world."
He said handling her a thousand bucks note.

Shocked by the money on her palm.
She was too confused to say a word,
Who was this strange man in a coat?
With auburn hair and French beard.

She asked her helper to take care of this shop,
And tip toed outside like a mouse.
She couldn't stand the curiosity any more,
And decided to follow this man to the house

She reached a dainty cottage soon,
And crossed the garden with quick strides.
Peeping though the window her mouth fell open,
When she raw the vision of inside.

Heena didn't know how to react,
She didn't understand her own feeling,
There lay a paralytic woman on the bed,
Motionless, staring at the ceiling.

The man walked in brightly smiling.
At the woman laying on the bed,
He slipped the bangles into her still wrist,
And gently kissed her on the forehead.

As the sunlight from the window fell on her wrist,
Colourful light made patterns in the ceiling up there,
"now you can see your gift shining at the time."
Happy Birthday Beautiful Maria may dear.

Heena slowly walked out of the gate,
And the tears made her eyelids quiver,
Now she knew that love was so much more.
Than the prices of Diamonds, Gold and Silver.